THE SEED IS SOWN

THE SEED IS SOWN

LEWIS I. MYERS, JR.

CONVENTION PRESS / NASHVILLE, TENNESSEE

The cover: Pastor Joseph Kamuti presides at a baptismal service of the Kathemboni Baptist Church in Kenya. PHOTO BY HAROLD CUMMINS.

Introduction

Agricultural terms and concepts often illustrate spiritual truths in the New Testament. There are several occasions when "planting a seed" is used to describe the growth of the church. Southern Baptists are a people committed to the church. We have been used of God to plant churches in our own homeland and in many places around the world.

No two of those places are exactly alike.

Just as churches in New York City differ from churches in Mobile, and the New Bethel Baptist Church, Ruraltown, USA, differs from the First Baptist Church of Capital City, the First Baptist Church, Barra da Tijuca, Brazil, differs from the Kathemboni Baptist Church in Kenya; and they both differ from the Kinoynoy Baptist Church in the Philippines. In this book we will look at how the seed of the gospel is planted in all these different kinds of places and how the church grows.

The New Testament speaks of a seed falling in the ground and dying in order to bear fruit. When the gospel seed sown by a foreign missionary grows, it does not produce a church like the one the missionary grew up in, but rather one that is suited to the needs of the people in the new land. The seed that is sown by a person from one culture must fall into the ground of the new culture, dying in order for a new plant to grow. This plant grows true to its rootage in the gospel kernel. There is no compromise of the truth of the gospel in the mature plant that results. The church flourishes in the cultural soil and climate in which it is planted.

Baptists have used dozens and perhaps even hundreds of methods in order to plant churches. Sometimes churches are planted

as Baptists emigrate from a large city into a homestead-type fron-
tier area. They begin as house churches, Bible study groups, Bible reading groups; through art galleries, radio or television,
disaster response, developmental ministry projects, hospitals, and
clinics, revivals and direct evangelism by career missionaries, national Christians and volunteers. The variety of places and the
variety of methods make church planting on a global basis a
beautiful mosaic of God's movement among his people.

In this volume only a few cases are selected to demonstrate
church planting, but they are representative of a much larger
whole—a body of believers called Baptists.

ONE
The Seed and the Grove

A kithembeo is a strange and eerie place. It is a grove of holy trees—a sacrifice place for the Wakamba* of Kenya. Large crowds gather there twice each year to participate in the sacrifice of goats and to pray for rain.

According to traditional African religion the goat must be selected with great care. He must be the finest of the flock and must be perfectly black. The slaughtering of the goat, the spilling of blood as sacrifice, is accompanied by great ceremony presided over by the Wakamba elders. Drums echo through the day and into the night, and dancers pound the parched ground with their feet, swaying to the frenzied beat of the drums. Excitement and anticipation are heightened and weariness staved off by the massive consumption of *pombe*. As the strong beer takes effect people feverishly offer prayers to the spirits of the grove to bring rain to the parched land.

Joseph Kamuti grew up near a kithembeo. He remembers well the ceremony and excitement of the great sacrifice days. He also remembers the abject poverty of his youth. Joseph and his family worked hard, but nothing they did seemed to push them very far beyond the edge of starvation. Where he lives, when the rains don't come and seed for the next season's crop is used for food this season, there is little hope. Starvation is a constant threat.

Joseph, as many young men in rural areas, decided to leave the village and go to the city. He went to Nairobi to look for work. Joseph was one of the fortunate young men. It took him a long time, but he finally found work in a meat packing plant which eventually brought security to him and his family.

---
*Kamba is the name of the tribe; *Mkamba* is singular—a member of the *Kamba* tribe; *Wakamba* is the plural form.

Joseph's move to Nairobi brought him even greater security. He became a Christian. His life was transformed and he became active in a nearby Baptist church.

The more Joseph's walk with the Lord deepened the more he grew uneasy about his home village. Finally he resigned his job and moved back near the kithembeo. He wanted to see a Baptist church there.

Back in his village, Joseph went from house to house talking with the people about Christ. He told Bible stories and invited people to repent and accept Christ. He went to other villages nearby. After a few weeks a small church was started with those who became believers. The seed was sown and the church planted.

The little band of Christians decided they needed a meeting house, so they secured a small plot of ground and built a mud and thatch house—right in front of the kithembeo!

The more the little church grew the more the elders and other adherents of the traditional African religion became vexed. Joseph wanted to "challenge the powers of Satan," writes Jackson Mativo, the current pastor of the church which was founded there. "So like Elijah in the Old Testament, he said to the elders that they could pray for rain but the gods of the grove would not answer. Then he would pray to the Living God and rain would fall. This happened exactly as he said, and this gave the young church a good beginning. God's power, you see, is very important to us in Africa. Now, today, you can see here our large, beautiful church building, and that place of goat sacrifice is abandoned and all of the elders have either died or been converted to Christ, praise God!"

The name of the church? Kathemboni—"at the place of sacrifice."

Kathemboni Baptist Church is the mother and grandmother church of dozens of churches among the Wakamba people.

Enter Harold and Betty Cummins

Harold grew up in a small town in south Arkansas. He says: "I had daily contact with black people. God was preparing me for Africa. Later, prior to appointment as a foreign missionary, I had experience in church planting in both North Carolina and California. While in California I was a teaching fellow at Golden

Missionary Harold Cummins and Joseph Kamuti lead a service of the Kambu Baptist Church, a sister of the Kathemboni Church.

Gate Baptist Seminary in the Department of Missions. There, also, God was preparing me to teach as I now do through seminary extension."

Harold and Betty were appointed in 1959, at first not to Africa but to East Pakistan (Bangladesh). Three years of service among rural people in Bangladesh followed. Then they were transferred to Kenya and had seven years among urban people in Nairobi, Kenya's captial.

David Masika, a Mkamba, became Cummins's good friend in Nairobi. David talked often of his tribe and their spiritual need and Cummins became more and more interested. He learned

Members of Parklands Baptist Church, Nairobi, Kenya, linger after Sunday morning worship services.

that there were almost two million of them and that they lived in the arid area of central Kenya. The Wakamba are an agricultural people, growing maize, beans, millet and a variety of vegetables and fruits. They also herd cattle, goats and sheep on their desert-like land dotted with scrubby bush.

The challenge was great. There were a few Baptist churches in the district of Ukambani, nine to be exact; but there was reason to believe the people would be responsive to the gospel. Poverty was rampant. The growth of the churches had been slow over the last decade. The Kathemboni Church and eight sister churches were led by pastors paid by foreign funds. Thus church growth was tied to the availability of foreign mission funds.

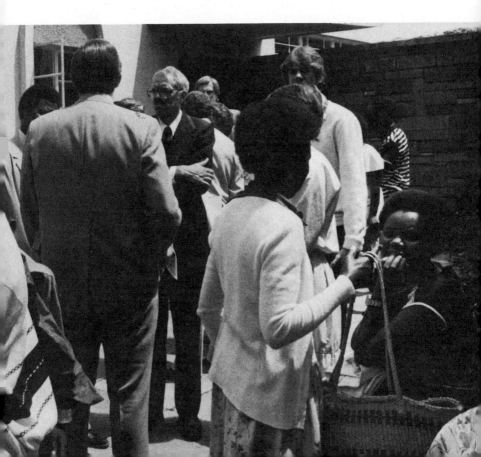

Ten Years of Church Growth

After ten years of following new guidelines and principles, those original nine churches have grown to over 120. What happened? What principles guided this growth? What programs developed?

First, the nine pastors and the missionary made a careful study of the Bible and evangelism. They discovered that God clearly intends for his churches to multiply by reproduction. As Cummins states: "Christ's teaching is alive with the excitement of growth. He spoke of fishers of men and of harvesters, of branches producing fruit and of light penetrating the darkness." These biblical studies showed the ten men clearly that they should be responsible co-workers with God, trained soldiers, faithful shepherds and entirely dependent upon the power of God's spirit.

Second, they worked out plans for planting many small new churches. Previous surveys in other places in Kenya had indicated that 74 percent of the members of a church live within one mile of that church's building. The ten men determined that they would plant churches three miles apart throughout the district. All the people, with few exceptions, walked to church. There is not one privately-owned vehicle per thousand people here. It was important to the people to have a church fairly nearby.

The African, or more specifically, the Wakamba sense of family pervades church life, and small churches have much of the "family flavor."

Cummins states: "To . . . implement the strategy, we needed to share widely the reasons for starting many new churches. We taught that this was necessary because of the rapid increase in population, because so many people—very, *very* many people are lost—because God loves the lost . . . that life itself is too short to be doing lesser things. We emphasized that churches helped to change lives and change villages, change families, change nations."

William and Emil Ngosi, members of the Kamba tribe, use a water filter system taught them by a missionary.

These are the plans Cummins and the nine pastors developed:
1. Pray and plan.
2. Enlist helpers.
3. Survey the areas.
4. Visit families.
5. Find a meeting place.
6. Begin the meetings.
7. Find and train a leader.

Third, the group determined to undergird the hoped-for church growth with continual on-the-job training for all new pastors. Theological Education by Extension (TEE) is the tool used to achieve this goal. All pastors are expected to enroll in TEE. There are currently 11 centers in the association. These centers

A TEE (Theological Education by Extension) class meets at Kisingo Baptist Church, where Harold Cummins passes out theology tapes.

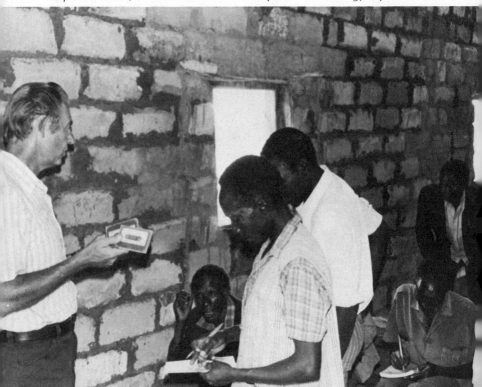

Women whose husbands are attending the TEE class join missionary Betty (Mrs. Harold) Cummins for activities and fellowship. (Left to right, Janet Julius Matuku, Tabitha Ngumu, Dorcas Kasuna, Cummins.)

are actually seminars for pastors. Programmed instruction texts designed for self-study are available in the Swahili language. These include basic biblical study and practical pastoral ministry studies. What are the advantages of this approach? It takes the seminary to the pastor. He learns while actively serving his church.

With this simple yet profound strategy in place, Cummins and the pastors set about to implement it. The question the pastors were soon faced with was "How will starting new churches help our church?" They could point to several factors; for example, a mother church that gives birth to a daughter church often experiences revival and renewal. God often blesses by bringing new people into the mother church as well.

A Family Affair

Thus new church planting became both a family affair and a cooperative effort. Cummins describes the process: "It was vital that families be reached for Christ and that even chains of families come to him. If the head of the family becomes a Christian,

The Wakamba consider music a vital part of worship, as indicated by this 40-member choir of Kambu Baptist Church.

then the whole extended family . . . is open to the gospel. . . . They share the gospel with other loved ones within their closeknit group. As more and more (people) are saved, new churches are born."

Christ's instruction was that the church "make disciples" *and* "teach them to observe the things I have commanded." Obedience demands that churches be planted *and* nurtured. The Ukambani South Baptist Association came into being for just that purpose: it was the organizational unit used to strengthen the churches. The pastors have promoted youth camps, Bible drills and quizzes, choir contests, writers' contests and speakers' con-

Daniel K. Munyau, pastor of Kariobangi Baptist Church, visits the neighborhood of church member Alice Njeri and her husband, Vidan Karani, who is not a Christian.

tests to train the youth. A tape ministry has provided study materials for the pastors and music for the congregations.

Music is very important to Africans and therefore is greatly emphasized in the churches. Bibles and prayer guides in the Kikamba language are used extensively.

Brother Jackson Mativo, who has watched the growth of the churches in the area from the beginning, has sharp insight into reasons for rapid growth. "At Kathemboni we have been from the beginning and still are a church of prayer. This prayer was combined with personal, direct witness to relatives. And still, today, we believe that prayer, much prayer, with Christians all together, is the secret of receiving God's power for God's work. There have been, however, two changes. First, TEE was introduced and we

Church leader Timothy Makaw reads scripture at Kambu Baptist Church.

got training. This has remade my ministry and greatly influenced the church. Second, missionary Cummins began to inspire and teach us more and more about church planting. We really got excited about evangelism! Our church is happy to be the mother of many children."

An elder of the Maasai tribe in Kenya "put down the stick" for God when he was more than 100 years old. Missionary Harold Cummins, left, baptized him.

But what about the folk around the grove who watched all this happen? James Muindi was one. "I was only 10 years old when I first heard about Jesus. It was here at the place of sacrifice. Some new Christians built a small mud church building. I started coming to Bible study. I looked around at those outside the church and saw much drunkenness, fighting, witchcraft, stealing and lying; and such sinners, I saw, had no real happiness. I came to know Jesus in a personal way and my life was changed. In time

Maasai women retain traditional clothing styles.

my mother, older brothers and sisters, one uncle and some aunts were all converted—all except my father, who is still not a Christian. Other relatives and neighbors here on this mountainside and down there in the valley became believers. We all became Christians.

"I say 'we' because we do things together as a family. What our relatives and clan members do is very important to each individual one of us. Our relationship with Christ and the church is in the context of our relating to each other. We decided one by one about Christ on our own. But you could also say we decided as a family. At Kathemboni our Christian roots, I think, are very strong."

Muindi has been recently involved in starting a new church. As choir director at Kathemboni he decided to use choir as an outreach tool. Capitalizing on the African interest in music he started having choir practice in people's homes. "Well, music is a witness and perhaps the best witness in Africa." Many persons have been won to the Lord and new churches started by Muindi and his choir outreach program.

Love Thy Neighbor

There is more to the story. The Maasai people, tribal neighbors of the Wakamba, were traditional enemies of the Wakamba. Battles were fought over cattle and land use. The Maasai, tall and willowy, wrapped in brightly colored robes, have begun hearing about the changes taking place among the Wakamba. They are beginning to desire Christ and to have his church planted among them. Currently there are seven churches among the Maasai where the Wakamba touch their neighbors. Recently 38 Maasai were baptized, including the wife of a chief and a 100-year-old man. God is still working his quiet miracles.

Harold Cummins says: "Once I was walking several steps behind a Maasai warrior. I began to talk by asking a question. 'Bwana, why is it that your people continue to live in darkness, or at least in the early dawn? Why have you rejected the light of Jesus?' The warrior turned and looked at me with eyes flashing like a Maasai spear and spoke words more memorable than the charge of a raging elephant. 'Reject it?' he said. 'Reject it? We have never rejected the light of Jesus. No one ever came to tell us.'"

TWO
The Seed and the Cup

Even if you have the availability of fresh fruit, vegetables and other farm products, $25 a year is not very much income for a farm family. Not even in Kinuskusan, Philippines. Living conditions are very poor and the sloping land makes farming difficult. Families have to move often because the fertile topsoil washes down the slopes during the monsoon rains. The plot that produced 20 bags of corn the first year produces about five the fifth year. So the pattern is "farm five years and move—or starve." Rural life cent

Typically children drop out of school in the second or third grade, having gone to school those two or three years hungry and dirty.

Anaclito Ando grew up like this. His fellow Bagobos (the tribe to which he belongs) found little comfort in their religion—he less than most. He saw little response to his plight from the spirits who were believed to inhabit the bamboo groves and banyan trees. Early in his life Ando decided he had more faith in himself and his strength than he did in those spirits.

Ando liked to fight; in fact he had quite a local reputation as a brawler-type boxer. He had even seriously considered becoming a professional boxer on a big-time scale. But he also gained an even greater reputation as a drinker—or perhaps more accurately, a drunkard.

He took a wife in order to father children. She could not have children; so, according to Bagobo tradition, she helped Ando pick out a second wife who *could* have children. They all lived together in the same house.

Ando was a leader in the community and was known as a progressive farmer—progressive by comparison only with those around him. The tighter his personal situation got the more desperate he became and the more he drank and fought. No hope could be found in the poor sloping land and none was offered by the spirit in the banyan tree. The decades of the fifties and sixties were hard and hopeless.

Enter Harold and Joyce Watson

Half a world away in Hattiesburg, Mississippi, Harold Watson was grappling with the fifties and sixties too. He earned extra money by working for farmers, chopping cotton and picking cotton. "Through my high school years I had to work hard and assume many responsibilities. I was active in clubs. I was president of the Future Farmers of America. I participated in many

Missionary Harold Watson, in hat, discusses goat raising at a seminar of the Baptist Rural Life Center at Kinuskusan, Mindanao, Philippines.

contests—parliamentary procedures, livestock judging, etc. Although I went to church, I did not mature as a Christian during those years as I should have done."

After graduating from high school, Harold joined the Air Force. During those four years in the Air Force his Christian commitment was strengthened and his vocational choice set toward agriculture. He had also been licensed to preach during this time. Little did he know that the Lord had a special purpose in the blend of preaching and agriculture! Four more years found Harold winding up a master of science in agricultural education degree. "My thesis was on agricultural mission work on foreign mission fields as sponsored by various religious boards. Through this study many of my philosophies about agricultural missions were formed."

By 1964 God had set the stage for Harold Watson to meet Anaclito Ando. Harold and Joyce were appointed for the Philippines as agricultural evangelists. By 1971 they had opened the Mindanao Baptist Rural Life Center.

The Mindanao Baptist Rural Life Center

From the very beginning the Rural Life Center has had as its purpose the planting and strengthening of churches. During the first 14 years of its history, over 30 churches have been planted in the area of the center. Harold explains the success of the center by answers to two basic questions: What goes on at or through the center? How does this produce churches?

"First of all, let me say that I do not believe that anyone comes to a saving knowledge of Christ through agriculture per se," Watson explains. "Agriculture cannot lift a person out of his sins and bring him in union with Christ, but we believe agricultural work helps in opening doors and demonstrating Christ's love.

"Some people preach Christ by using words, putting them together into sentences in a way that people can understand. We have used agriculture, putting events together in such a way that through them people can see Christ."

During Watson's first several years in the Philippines, early impressions from that M.S. thesis at Mississippi State University were cemented. He found that one of the main problems was getting the farmer to see what he was talking about. He also wanted to be very sure that what he was trying to teach was not theory but something practical that really worked.

The Mindanao Baptist Rural Life Center was founded as a base "(1) to test various cropping systems, to test various techniques of growing crops or animals, and, in some cases, to do light research work; (2) to bring farmers in and actually show them what was being done." The title "Rural Life Center" was chosen with care. "We called it a Rural Life Center because we did not want it to be thought of as an experimental station or a demonstration farm, but as a center that dealt in rural life, both physical and spiritual."

All programs of the center, including those that are extensions from the center, have a basic evangelistic and church planting dimension to them. This has been true from the beginning and this is where Watson's and Ando's paths crossed.

Adjacent to the center is the Baptist camp, Mt. Carmel. The first Sunday the Watsons were in residence at Kinuskusan they had worship services for their family and the small staff of the center. They met in a building at the camp. "Then we went around and invited other people to come. They were curious about what was happening. Why were Americans here farming? What kind of project was this?" The curiosity spread to some of the tribesmen, the Bagobos, who lived in the area and some of them came to see.

As Watson followed up with visits in the villages from which the people had come, he became aware that they were interested in having a class in corn production. He relates: "I went there,

Journeyman Glenn K. Turner demonstrates use of the "A" frame to level the contour of land on a hillside of the Philippines.

contacted the leader in the community, and he helped us call the people together. I told him what we wanted to do was help them have a better way of life both physically and spiritually." The plan was to start with a class in corn production and then have a Bible study class.

One of the leaders who came to the corn production class and the Bible class was Anaclito Ando. "Christ touched his life in an unusual way. Almost overnight his life was changed."

Within two months 14 other people had also professed faith in Christ and had been baptized. The Kinoynoy Baptist Church was planted. The distance from Hattiesburg, Mississippi, to Mindanao, Philippines, suddenly didn't seem very far.

The little church met in the home of one of its members. They

Fabula Calib, a Rural Life Center leader who holds extension classes, lectures at a meeting of the Christian Farmers' Club, Kinoynoy Baptist Church.

soon outgrew it and needed a building of their own. The church leaders decided they must erect such a building, but they were poor farmers on the edge of poverty themselves. Where would the money come from? Watson suggested, "You could build something like the house you live in right in your village without cost. Bamboo and thatch are easily available."

The little church quickly agreed that he was right, but they still had a problem. How could they secure land? Anaclito Ando, only slightly less poor than the rest, said that he would donate the land for their church. It was done!

Working with that small but growing band of Christians, Watson and the staff at the farm helped them contour some of their land to prevent erosion and set up a cooperative to buy fertilizer and generally improve farming techniques. It's been ten years now since this church, the first resulting from the extension activity of the center, was planted and the "seed planted is bearing fruit."

"Now the children are able to go to school," Watson says. "No more are they dropping out in the second and third grade. I think one of the greatest tributes to this particular church was from the local school teacher, who was not a Christian: 'There really has been a difference in the children from the Kinoynoy area. They keep coming to school, they have food, they are clean and they even pray in school.' So lives really did begin to change. Their whole pattern of living, of drinking, wild parties and violence has changed."

Church Planting in Mindanao

This new church was not content, however, just to see the change occur in their village. When it was less than one year old, members started outreach in another area. They found their natural contact with relatives and friends in other communities to be a channel through which to communicate the gospel. One such area was Eman, four kilometers away. People there responded to the Christians' witness. With Watson's help, the Kinoynoy church started a Bible study there and later an agricultural class as well. The reverse order from the Kinoynoy church beginning, the Eman church simply started at the point of expressed need that was stimulated by those who had experienced changed lives and believed they should share God's love with their neighbors.

In Eman, as well as in many other communities in the area, many religions have made promises, but in the end none of them were fulfilled. A total lack of confidence in religion was rampant and some hostility toward religion was evident. Watson says: "When we get the peoples' confidence through our interest in their agriculture, they are willing to open their lives to us and learn the things we are teaching. We have found that once people accept you as a person who is trying to help them, they automatically open their lives to you, and they begin to believe what you

Evalyn Eman, a BOOST (Baptist Out of School Training) graduate receives further instruction from her supervisor, Tito Felongco, in her home village.

Watson talks with a young couple of the Bagobo tribe in front of the home of an ill Filipino lay pastor he has just visited.

are saying."

A chain reaction of church planting was begun and the movement continues. Watson: "In the early '70s when we first began to start the churches—the one in Kinoynoy, then the one in Eman—the Eman church then began to reach out and start another work. We felt these new churches needed to interact with each other so we organized the Bagobo Baptist Fellowship. This was the forerunner of the association. Each month we met. The people walked in, brought their lunches and we met together. We had classes in agriculture, doctrine, music, and ended with an inspirational message. When the number of churches reached 12, we organized the Bagobo Baptist Association.

"Now the association is sponsoring its own evangelist from the contributions of the churches. So from this one man, Anaclito Ando, who was one of the first to step out and make a profession of faith, have now come over 30 churches."

Ongoing Work of the Rural Life Center

The Rural Life Center continues to play an important role in this expansion. First, the agricultural extension classes continue. These classes are not only excellent methods of outreach into new villages and communities, but the results of the teaching in terms of better agricultural production are providing stability for the farmer and thus for the new churches that are developing. The fact that cash contributions from the churches are supporting an associational evangelist is testimony to their growing financial strength.

A Christian Farmers' Club has been formed, designed specifically to help strengthen these rural churches. Some of these churches do not have pastors because they have no money to pay them. Better agricultural methods are introduced through the Christian Farmers' Club. Several churches have been able to strengthen themselves because of the resulting income coming

Two BOOST trainees work their garden plot near their quarters at the Rural Life Center, Kinuskusan.

into the churches through improved income of members.

Second, guests, observers, and participants in classes come to the center in a steady stream. Around 6,000 persons per year visit the center, and an additional 1,500 are trained in seminars. As the visitors come for tours of the center "we relate to them why we are here. We are Christians and are concerned about the total person. We believe God is concerned about the total person. He is concerned about a people's health—that they develop mentally and intellectually," Watson says.

"As we do seminar work here (we have at least one seminar a week in various areas of agriculture), we hold Bible studies. Each person who attends a seminar will come in contact with the gospel. Through this we have had many persons come to know Christ. We must slant the presentation of the gospel and the method of eliciting response to the group. Some of them are farmers who are uneducated and can hardly read and write. Some are college professors. We even had one group who were presidents of agricultural schools across the Philippines. But every group gets a simple presentation of the gospel."

Third, the BOOST program brings students to the center for study. In working with the churches in Bagobo Baptist Association, Watson discovered that the churches were peopled by Christians with no experience in the faith—new Christians. He started an informal Bible institute. Out of this Bible institute grew the BOOST project, Baptist Outside-of-School Training. Many young people come to the BOOST program and have been taught agriculture and Bible. About one-fourth of the curriculum is Bible study and about three-fourths is agriculture. These young adults then can go back to their churches, teach Sunday School and lead singing. Many have gone to other villages to start work.

Calvin Fox, another Southern Baptist missionary, works with the BOOST trainees and has developed a program of evangelism

Journeyman Glenn K. Turner checks pineapple plants with BOOST trainee Serio Esteban at the Rural Life Center.

and church planting with them. He views himself only as their counselor because they are fully capable of handling the evangelism now. Those who have gotten BOOST training go back to their villages as farmers who know how to preach as well as how to farm.

Fox started with some ideas and a few guidelines for planting new churches and developing a community economic base. These guidelines have been tested and revised several times and have been developed into a full and detailed plan for new church and community development. He says: "This can best be defined as community development. I do not believe you can have proper community development without a developed New Testament church in that community."

Fox sees their plan moving through four phases:

(1) Preparing a village for evangelism through home Bible studies.

(2) Planting a church and training leaders. This leadership training would include sending one or two promising leaders for BOOST training.

(3) Developing the planted church through evangelistic campaigns.

(4) Using BOOST graduates to open new work by Bible study and using their own farms for demonstrations.

As each new church develops it will reproduce itself, becoming mother and grandmother to many children and grandchildren.

Watson, reflecting on the past and looking toward the future, comments: "The basic concept that we have had of using agriculture to open doors, to win people's confidence and to simply say 'Christ loves you and we want to demonstrate that love,' we found to be the kind of concept we want to keep on following. Christians come to us and say: 'Well, we have planted a new church. We went over that mountain there to another village and

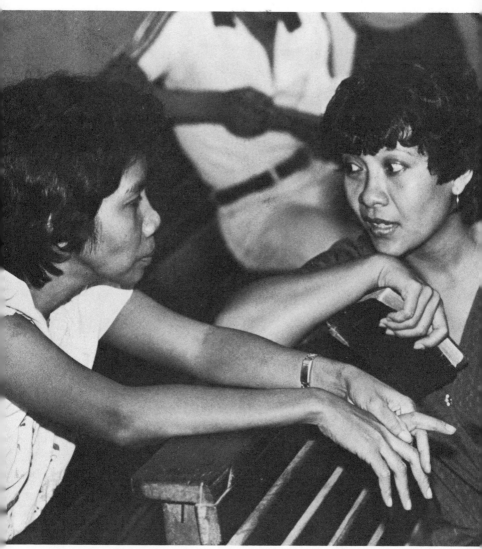

Two members of Dadiangas Baptist Church, General Santos, Philippines, visit after a worship service.

we have been holding Bible classes. We have just baptized 20 people and a church is planted there.' So we started a few and demonstrated that they too have a responsibility in evangelizing their own people. The work has progressed and moves on."

Yes, the movement continues. The spark struck by the Watson-Ando encounter still glows.

THREE
The Seed and the Home

Guidebooks, with indisputable authority, announce that the city of Ashkelon in Israel was founded by South African Jews in A.D. 1953, and they very properly add that it was already old when the Israelites were in bondage in Egypt. In fact, it was the Afridar section of modern Ashkelon that was founded in A.D. 1953; Ashkelon itself was first mentioned in history in Egyptian letters around 1900 B.C. Indeed, the city is old, but it wears its age well. Long white beaches, low green hills, intensely blue sea, warm African winds and new housing developments at every hand are some images with which the visitor leaves. To go to Ashkelon is to see a city rising before one's eyes.

But to go to Ashkelon as a "seeing believer" is to observe something else—something as old as the New Testament and as new as today's world.

House churches are as old as the New Testament. Paul frequently greeted "the church in your house" as he wrote to encourage the early Christians in Rome, Corinth and Colossae and as he wrote to Philemon.

Today, in almost every country where Baptists are at work, the house meeting approach is being used with great effectiveness. Large churches scattered around the world had their beginning as a home Bible study or home fellowship. Many mother churches use the homes of members as outreach points that eventually grow into churches.

But this ministry in Ashkelon today is unique in Israel. To understand what God is doing in the lands of the Bible through home ministry requires looking at church from a viewpoint different from our traditional one.

The ruins in the background and the sycamore trees tie this area of Ashkelon, Israel, to biblical times.

Enter James and Betty Smith

Jim and Betty Smith moved their family to Ashkelon in 1967 and committed themselves to Christian witness through home ministry. Jim says: "In order for the sharing of the Christian faith to take place, Christian believers must reckon with the grim episodes of historical anti-Semitism and seek to present a true Christianity in the midst of distrust. This Christianity does not seek to bring change from without but to transform from within. It lives among the people, shares in their daily life and gradually gains acceptance. It is a Christianity which flows from a Christ-centered home, manifests itself in quiet and friendly ways and is wholly characterized by patience, perseverance and good will."

Gradually the trust grew about which Jim Smith talks, and believers were added to the "family."

A typical meeting of the Ashkelon home ministry lasts an hour or so. The usual Middle East custom of a time of fellowship with light refreshments and conversation begins the evening. Various musical instruments are brought by the believers for a time of song and praise. Prayer requests are shared, and the group engages in intercessory prayer for each other.

Bible study is a favorite time for the believers and their friends who come with them. Bibles in several languages are opened for the study. Since the establishment of the state of Israel in 1948, Jewish people have immigrated there from over 90 nations in the world. It is common to need Bibles in several languages to accommodate individuals who have not yet mastered the national language of Hebrew or who prefer to read the Bible in their own native tongue.

Rebecca and Jacob (not their real names, and not a married couple) are always there—but they got there from very different places, traveling very different roads.

Jacob had been looking for a caring family for a long time. An American Jew, he had come to Israel to get away. He ended up at

Missionary James W. Smith views scripture on monuments at Ashkelon.

Eilat in the '70s, living on the beach and scavenging for food, clothing, shelter—and drugs. His search for a caring family attached him to a colony of "hippies," but there still was no satisfaction.

One day he stumbled into the tent of a group of believers on the beach. They witnessed to him, and he came to know the Lord—and later he came to know Jim Smith.

Jacob became an Israeli citizen, served in the army and was stationed at a base near Ashkelon. He and his bride are faithful in the home ministry. He speaks openly of his faith and recently gave his testimony before a Jewish audience at a concert of Christian music in Ashkelon.

Jacob at last has found a caring family.

Rebecca is a Jewish woman from Holland. She escaped from Nazi pressure by living under the deck of a canal barge, where she was hidden by a Christian captain. She and her husband and two daughters live on a kibbutz (collective settlement) near Ashkelon. Her drive for freedom made her a pioneer freedom fighter. She also had an unquenchable thirst for truth. Since the kibbutz was small, it was not difficult for Rebecca to meet Ellen. Ellen was a student of Hebrew in the kibbutz language school. She was an active, witnessing Christian. Ellen won Rebecca to the Lord and also led her to Jim Smith.

After Ellen left, Rebecca was the only Christian left on the kibbutz, and she was a secret believer. Feeling the need for Christian fellowship and Bible study, she became a part of the Ashkelon home ministry. She now talks openly about her faith with her husband and daughters. She has even become bold enough to request the kibbutz vehicle to bring her to the Ashkelon meetings. She reads widely and is capable of counseling new believers. Jim Smith reflects: "Rebecca was restless and miserable until

James Smith, 2nd from right, visits Jewish friends on a kibbutz. This family emigrated to Israel from Holland years ago.

she found the peace that Jesus gives. She looks upon the home ministry family as her larger family." In this family Rebecca has found truth and freedom.

But all of this did not "just happen." Concepts of ministry were hammered out through experience, barriers were overcome through love, and new light was brought through a turning point experience.

Emergence of Home Ministry in Ashkelon

"In August 1967 when I moved from Nazareth to Gaza and began living part-time in Ashkelon, I learned that the traditional missionary methods used successfully among Arabs would not work in an all-Jewish city. When I opened an office and put up a sign in Ashkelon, the extreme reaction from Orthodox Jews taught me to try another approach. They repeatedly broke into my office, scattered my books and papers, tore down my sign and spit on the door," Smith says.

At this point, he started a reflective process on the nature of the gospel and the nature of the barriers to be overcome.

The Middle East is full of barriers—political, social and re-ligious. The Bible teaches that barriers are to be overcome by presence and by love. This is the essence of the Incarnation. Just as Jesus was incarnate, visibly alive with a body, and lived within a culture, so must the gospel be incarnate in the life of a believer who is willing to live it out in the midst of a culture. This is presence and love. Beginning with this truth, Smith's concept of the ministry gradually was formed.

The decision by the Baptist mission in Israel to enter the all-Jewish city of Ashkelon was not made because there was a core of believers who requested them to come help. It was completely a venture of faith on the part of the James Smith family and the supporting mission. It was a desire to share the gospel of the Lord Jesus Christ in a way which would effectively communicate to

Jews. The effort was not an extension of any church, nor were there any of the usual aids, such as a group of believers or any Christian institution to support the ministry.

The barriers the Smiths faced were barriers erected mainly by Jewish interpretation of Christian terminology.

The word *Christian* is filled with threatening overtones from the Crusades, the Inquisition, the Russian pogroms and the Holocaust. Anyone neither Jew nor Muslim is considered a Christian.

Missionary is used by rabbis and other religious leaders to refer to a person who behaves deceitfully and gives material inducements to bring in converts.

Church is considered to be the organized body which has caused much suffering to the Jewish nation, and the church building is the physical symbol of that oppression.

For many Jews in Ashkelon, the presence of a Baptist family offered the first opportunity for a positive and personal encounter with Christians.

It became obvious to the Smiths that any ministry which would make this positive and personal interaction possible must avoid reinforcing the old barriers. The home ministry is built upon two factors. One is the study of the Bible. Bible study, as an academic pursuit, is an intellectually approved enterprise in Israel—particularly the study of the Old Testament. The prospect of participating in a study of the Scriptures does not erect barriers for the Jews.

The second factor is the pivotal one on which the home ministry is built. The Bible teaches that Christ Jesus dwells in the heart of the believer by the power of the Holy Spirit. Therefore, the Body of Christ is to be manifested in the lives of believers who continue to live in an unbelieving community. No building, which would raise red flags of old barriers, is necessary. No in-

Visiting James and Betty Smith are next-door neighbors, Ruth and Chaim Yashin, a Jewish family from the conservative tradition. The two families work together to bring Arabs and Jews together as friends.

stitutional structure, again the red flags, is required. Jim Smith comments, "The family unit is itself the church structure, and the Bible study group is an outgrowth of the family's personal faith."

The actual setting up of the group began with the Baptist family (the Smiths) securing property, moving into the community and studying the makeup and the sensitivities of the people who resided there. The family became aware of the spiritual standing of their individual neighbors and noted their interest and participation in the religious and cultural life of the community.

More than a year was needed to locate those who had some degree of interest in Bible study. The ministry from the home began with Christian visitors, volunteers in the kibbutzim, and with others who were seeking Christian worship and Bible study. Through this process, the Jews around the Smith family in Ashkelon came to regard them as the warm family next door whose activities did not pose a threat to them.

After contacting those who became seekers and some known believers in the area, the Smiths invited these people into their home for Bible study and prayer. Smith states, "It must be emphasized that all the contacts were personal encounters; there were no posters, mailouts or advertisements and no visible house-to-house survey."

The home Bible study began around the dining room table for

James and Betty Smith have song books and inspirational books for use when friends come to their home for worship and to discuss their faith in light of the Jewish religion.

the few who sought it. Gradually, as the number increased, additional space was adjoined to the house in the form of a library and a meeting room, with the latter furnished much like a family living room.

Just as the Bible study group takes the form of family and becomes the extension of the ministry of a Baptist family, the fol-

Living at Petah Tiqva, Israel, is the Choresh family, Jewish believers who attend the Baptist church at Baptist Village. Betty and James Smith especially enjoy visiting the family at Christmas. Left to right are Odeliyah; her father, Yaacov, a music teacher, Moriel; Esther; and oldest daughter, Naama; and the Smiths.

low-up activities are also the responsibility of that family. Converts and candidates for baptism must be carefully nurtured since there is no other Christian guidance for them in the community. Literature for personal growth, devotion and Bible study is made available to them. Discipleship programs, such as MasterLife, and some audiovisual materials are introduced into the follow-up program as needed. In order for the new believers to get a sense of community with the larger family of Christians, they visit Christian centers throughout the country. This helps them to become acquainted with other believers and strengthens

their faith by letting them know they are a part of a larger movement that has begun to spread in many different parts of Israel.

Now back to Jacob and Rebecca.

They have to be extremely cautious in sharing their faith and
inviting persons to share in the home ministry. They have
learned that one-on-one type witness is the most fruitful and recalls fewer old barriers.

Jacob participates and sometimes leads in discussion groups in
the home ministry. His belief in having found a caring home is so
deep he likely will be the leader of a home ministry in the future.

Rebecca often has seekers come to her in her kibbutz home,
and she shares with them as they walk through the fields of the
kibbutz. Her husband has become more tolerant of her faith,
though he and the daughters are not yet believers. She effectively
shares the truth and freedom which she has found in Christ.

Efficient church planting is taking place in Ashkelon. Without
buildings, the church has been planted there in the form of home
ministry. The results? Real, vital and viable Christian witness and
ministry in a positive, personal and barrier-free environment.

FOUR
The Seed and The Windowbox

Planting is done differently in the narrow confines of high-rise condominiums from the way it is done in the wide spaces of rural farmlands. In the former, flowers bloom and greenery flourishes in windowboxes or rooftoop urns. In the latter, endless rows of terraces stretch to the horizon—green with the growth of the season. Planting in the windowbox is an urban experience.

People who plot population trends predict that by the year A.D. 2000 the world will be more than 50 percent urban. At that time there will be over 400 cities in the world with 1,000,000 or more residents and five of them will have more than 20,000,000 each. This increased urbanization brings, among all the positive dynamics, some distressing negative implications.

As people move to the city from their rural upbringing, the traditional family structures come under stress. Crime becomes more heavily concentrated, life more and more impersonal, pollution more oppressive, and food supply increasingly more complicated. Rural community values and restraints are often lost.

A very different kind of planting must take place as the seed of the gospel is sown in the urban windowbox.

One of those sprawling urban centers is Rio de Janeiro in Brazil. Just the mention of Rio conjures up all sorts of exotic images! Sugarloaf Mountain, standing like a sentinel over Rio's exquisite harbor, lingers in the mind of would-be tourists. The trolley ride to the top affords an everchanging panorama of azure blue waters, sparkling white sands, verdant mountains, sprawling cities of Rio and Niteroi, slum shacks stacked up the steep mountainside, high-rise condominiums sprouting like giant index fingers along

A lonely, elderly man stares through Brazilian eyes at a Brazilian side-walk; but the same hopelessness and despair can be seen in eyes of people throughout the world to whom Southern Baptists seek to bring the gospel.

a narrow spit of land between the sea and inland basin, and the constant motion of traffic on all visible thoroughfares.

Two of the beach areas bear familiar names—Copacabana and Ipanema. High-rise apartments and condominiums are the rule of the day. Some are so exclusive that entry by nonresidents is highly controlled. Recently a condominium was sold for slightly over $1,000,000. Expensive automobiles are liberally sprinkled through these neighborhoods. It is not unusual to see several chauffeur-driven Rolls Royces in a row outside an exclusive apartment complex.

Enter Elizabeth Oates

Elizabeth Oates, missionary and director of the Baptist Institute of Religious Education in Rio, often took guests from North America to a beach area. Her interest was stirred each time she went to the beaches of the Barra da Tijuca. "I would think to myself, why can't Baptists do something out here?" she recalls. A missionary colleague, Jerry Key, kept urging her to be the one. The church he was pastor of wanted to sponsor a ministry at the Barra. "Me—start new work? I am not the type." But the Lord continued to probe her mind and she finally said "I'll go."

On March 13, 1978, Elizabeth Oates, Jorge Rodrigues, a Brazilian seminary student, and Wilce Prota, a student at the Baptist Institute of Religious Education, convenanted together to do all they could to sow the seed of the gospel in this area. Previous ministry by Baptists there, which had been discontinued as leadership changed, produced some religious census cards that offered a beginning point.

The three had made their commitment; they had some names and addresses in hand. Now what could be done? The first thought of renting a house or apartment as center of work was quickly discarded because the rent for the cheapest available place was over $1,000 a month!

This view of Copacabana Beach is mirrored at several of the beaches of Rio de Janeiro, Brazil.

Two focuses emerged for the ministry: a vigorous visitation effort and dynamic home Bible studies. Funneling into these two prongs the Lord used many events and people in a variety of places to bring about the organizing of the First Baptist Church of Barra da Tijuca. A Baptist church in North America, a pair of young adults from Texas, a Texas-Brazil partnership mission, several missionaries, students at the Rio Baptist Seminary and the Baptist Institute of Religious Education—all were used of God's spirit to plant his church. But we are a little ahead of our story.

Home Bible Study
in Brazil

On the initial visitation thrust by Elizabeth, Jorge and Wilce, they met Dona Virginia, who agreed to start a Bible study in her home. Virginia was a new believer. Her home was very simple but she graciously opened it, and the first Bible study was begun.

One Sunday as they gathered for Bible study at Virginia's home, she told Elizabeth about meeting a couple as they waited in line at a bank. Señor Francisco and his wife Dona Aldimira had just moved back to Brazil from New Jersey, where they had become believers. What was more, they were Baptists! A Bible study group was soon started in their home.

Later, another student at the Baptist Institute of Religious Education was added to the team as Hortencia da Costa started visitation in the adjacent community of Largo da Barra. Soon a home Bible study was begun there.

In the midst of affluence sits the economically deprived and spiritually needy area of Tijuinha. A Sunday morning Bible study was begun there.

After weeks of cultivation Dona Wilce Wanderly agreed for a home Bible study to be held in her home in the Barra. She was Baptist but had been out of church for 25 years. The first study was started in August 1978. A Sunday evening worship service was also begun in her home, and the first Christmas celebration of this group of new believers was held there!

Bible studies were now sprinkled throughout the area. Some met in the evenings, some on weekends. Some (especially for children) were on weekdays. Some groups were small and some were large. Faithfully the seed of the gospel was being sown in the windowboxes.

Elizabeth and her co-workers sat down to evaluate. Conclusion: "There is no unifying element to the work." They started

Hortensia da Costa, who attended Baptist Institute of Religious Education, where Elizabeth Oates taught, leads a Bible club for children in the home of a recent convert.

Elizabeth Oates (left) attends Bible study in the home of former spiritist Wilda Wonderly.

reaching for a way to begin to build a sense of community among all those studying the Bible in the different homes without destroying the dynamic of outreach by forcing premature centralization.

Texas-Brazil Partnership

Elizabeth reflects on those days. "A turning point came in the work as a result of the Texas-Brazil partnership mission. A crusade was to be held in Rio in November 1980. Because Jerry Key, who was then pastor of the mission, is a teacher at the seminary and I am director of Baptist Institute of Religious Education and November is the last month of the school year, we never thought of participating in the crusade. Without our knowledge, someone doing the Rio state level planning had listed our congregation as one of the participating churches. How were we going to have a crusade without an adequate place to meet?"

At about that time Dona Wilde moved to a new home in the Barra. Next to her house was a small office building which belonged to a spiritist. Surely the use of this building could not be secured for Christian worship from a spiritist! With a great deal of prayer and a little trepidation Señor Abreu was approached about using his building for the week's crusade meetings. He agreed to the use of it—without charge!

Doors started opening that had previously been shut as preparations were made for the crusade meetings. Invitations to the meetings were printed and permission was given for the believers to put them in mailboxes all over the Barra. Many of the highrise complexes and condominiums which before had been closed to them allowed the Baptists to put invitations in the mailboxes of all the residents.

The week of preaching by the Texas team produced a great deal of excitement among the believers; numbers of persons were won to faith in Jesus Christ, and many made first-time commitments

Seminary student Rui Cleber witnesses on a beach of Rio de Janeiro, Brazil.

to the gospel. Reflecting on the sense of community that emerged, Elizabeth recalls: "The thrilling thing about the week of revival services was that the people with whom we worked in all the different areas of the Barra met each other. . . . also several people accepted Christ. The team from Texas did a great job! Partnership missions was working for us."

At the end of the week they sat down to evaluate. The results had been so great that the group was now too large for Señor Francisco's home where the Sunday evening worship had been moved after outgrowing Dona Wilde's home. What must be done? Again, the decision had two focuses: continue the home Bible studies all over the Barra and negotiate with Señor Abreu to rent the office building for worship meetings. "We asked Señor Abreu if he would rent us the office space. He said 'No, you can keep meeting here free of charge.' We were not allowed to print the address on brochures, but we could invite people. At last we had a larger place!"

One of the things that Elizabeth and her team had discovered from the very beginning was that the youth of the Barra swarmed to the beaches during the week when crowds from other parts of Rio were less likely to be there. Help in the area came when two Mission Service Corps volunteers from Texas arrived to minister to the youth. Robert Doyle and Eva Cheatham, the MSCers, teamed with two Brazilian seminary students and students from the Baptist Institute of Religious Education in the weekday beach ministry and the weekend church ministry.

Robert grew up in Brazil, a son of missionaries, and speaks Portuguese. Eva is an outdoors person and sports enthusiast. Staying in the homes of Brazilians, these two ministered there for almost a year. They tossed frisbees, a novel thing at the time to Brazilian youth, with the young beach crowd. They made friends this way and let conversations "drift" toward religion and the ministry of the new church. Many youth were touched and channeled into the new congregation.

By June 1982 a small building had been constructed and dedicated. It was on property made available by the Rio State Convention. This was the First Baptist Church of Barra da Tijuca. Shortly after it was organized, Juarez Mendes, a seminary student, was called to be the pastor.

Getting the building was an important step. Not only was the office building which the congregation had been using now far

Eva Cheatham, Robert Doyle and Elizabeth Oates check the view from the church site (left to right).

too small, but the fact that the owner, who had given them the use of the building, did not allow them to print that address on publicity materials had limited the advertising the group could do. Elizabeth comments on the dedication of the church's own building, "How marvelous it was at last to have a home and an address!"

Seeking and Teaching

Looking back on the planting of the seed of the gospel in this urban windowbox, Elizabeth summarizes: "Among the first

Missionary Elizabeth Oates visits the site where First Baptist Church, Barra da Tijuca, Brazil, now stands with Robert Doyle and Eva Cheatham, Mission Service Corps representatives from Texas.

things . . . done after getting moved [into the new church] was the putting up of signs at strategic points indicating the way to the church. It would really be interesting to see how many of the present membership have been brought to the church by those signs. Most of those who were brought by the signs were believers who had been out of church for many years. Somehow in their

moving to the Barra the Lord used those signs to touch their hearts. However, the main key to the growth and development of the work has been consistent visitation and Bible study programs. It is going, going, going and going again and again to enlist people and to witness. It's not an easy way, but it is the way the Lord has honored at the Barra."

The First Baptist Church of Barra da Tijuca is a strong and growing church. It is self-supporting and gives substantial sums to the Brazil Baptist Convention's home and foreign mission offerings. What dynamics brought it into existence?

First, the right people were in place. Elizabeth, the catalyst, had never started new work, could not spend much time out of doors on the beach because of cataract surgery and contact lenses, had a full-time assignment as administrator of the Baptist Institute of Religious Education; but she was committed to starting work in the Barra. Dona Wilde moved back into active church life and negotiated the use of the office building. Mr. and Mrs. Francisco had just moved back to Brazil after having become Christians in a Baptist church in New Jersey and formed a vital part of the new work. The Texas crusade team and the two

Pastor Eliel de Freitas Cabral (right), a student at Equatorial Baptist Theological Seminary at the time of this photo, talks with a member of New Canaan Baptist Church, Belem, Brazil.

Students of South Brazil Baptist Theological Seminary continue a class-room discussion.

Mission Service Corps volunteers made significant contributions at turning points in the development of the church. The seminary and Baptist Institute of Religious Education students made themselves available and proved to be just the right blend in the formation of a strong team. When permission to build the building was denied, a dedicated, determined layman proved to be in position to negotiate with the zoning commission and secure permission to build. All along the way the right people were in place.

Again, the time was right and the timing of events advantageous to the growth of the church. Elizabeth and the team started work there just at the time when Mr. and Mrs. Francisco had returned. Dona Virginia was in a bank at just the right time to meet them and arrange to visit in their home. When many home Bible studies emerged with no cohesion to pull them together, the Texas team came. Mrs. Wanderly moved next door to an available building and was able to secure it in time for use during the crusade. Finally, when publicity for the initial evangelistic crusade was needed, the church members received permission to put handbills in mailboxes. The cadence of events was at just the right beat.

As increased urbanization takes place and people live in the impersonal atmosphere of high-rise, controlled-access apartment buildings and condominiums, the patient and personal touch of visitation often proves to be the breath of fresh air the Spirit uses to strike a responsive chord among the people. The Barra was no exception. Drawing people toward the Savior through Bible study was basic. The believers who emerged out of this process are strong in their belief and Bible-based in their convictions. The personal touch with the Word of God once again proved to be the right approach.

After a furlough in North America, Elizabeth returned to worship with the Barra church. "Last Sunday night the pastor was talking about the new work we needed to open farther down the beach. . . . I all but got cold chills. I thought to myself, 'Lord, will I have the courage to go through all this again—the seeking and the teaching?' Then I knew deep in my heart that as the Lord gave me strength to work with the first work at the Barra, he would give me strength to begin a second one."

FIVE
The Seed Falls . . . and Dies

"Except a corn of wheat fall in the ground and die, it abideth alone" (John 12:24). Southern Baptist missionaries and the Christians and leaders in countries where they serve have as their purpose to engage in "evangelism that results in churches." This simple phrase often distinguishes what Southern Baptists are about in their mission programs from the programs of other mission groups and societies.

Evangelism That Results in Churches

First, the focus is evangelism. The basic thrust of the New Testament is that Christ died to redeem, and that his redemptive death is for all persons everywhere. God entrusted to his church this precious gospel seed with the intent that it should be planted everywhere.

One growing idea that has found fertile ground in the minds of some is that because God is a God of love he surely will not allow good people anywhere to perish. This type of universalism, that a 'God of Love' ultimately will save everybody—especially the person who lives by me because he is such a good neighbor, blunts the edge of commitment to evangelism. Indeed, the New Testament speaks to the issue of God's caring love. It is not his will that any should perish but that all should come to repentance (2 Pet. 3:9). Paul also speaks to the issue of how God has planned that his salvation should be known to everyone. Everyone who calls on the name of the Lord will be saved. "But how shall they call on him in whom they have not believed, and how shall they believe in him of whom they have not heard, and how shall they hear without a preacher?" (Rom. 10:13-14).

Missionaries in partnership with Baptists of other countries engage in education, health care, relief, agriculture, administration, preaching, rural and urban development, music, publications and many other ministries; but the basic thread that runs through them all is commitment to share the love of God in Christ—to evangelize!

Second, the arena is church. Alan R. Tippett says in his book, *Church Growth and the Word of God*, "One of the unscriptural

Bina Borde, director of the Senter C. Crook Christian Student Center, finds abundant opportunity to talk with students who come by the center for recreation and "just to visit."

twists of contemporary theology, which . . . hinders the actual growth of the church, is the idea of a 'churchless ministry,' the adequacy of merely 'being a Christian out there in the world' without the need for a specific worshipping fellowship." Southern Baptist mission efforts are directed toward the planting and nurturing of New Testament style churches in all the lands where missionaries work. It is not the intent to leave scattered, unrelated individual Christians isolated from each other and the broader sustaining fellowship of the "body of Christ."

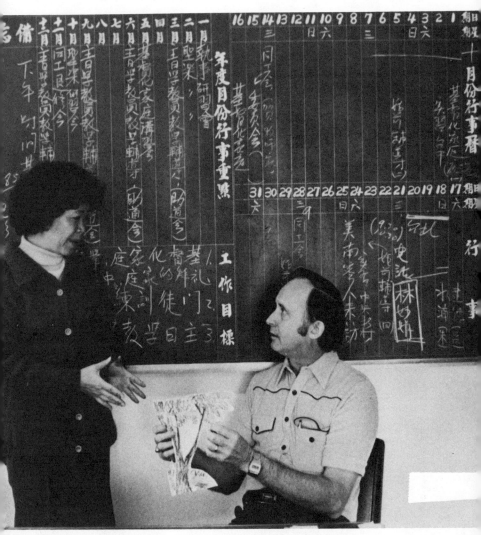

Missionary Charles C. Hardie and Le How, an artist and member of a Baptist church, make plans in the church training center, Grace Baptist Church, Taichung, Taiwan. Hardie is a discipleship consultant.

A great deal of missionary effort is spent in training national Christians and leaders because of the belief that they often are in a much better position to evangelize among their fellow countrymen than are persons coming in from outside that culture. It is also true that the church provides discipleship opportunities, a nurturing system, encouragement dynamics, and an appropriate arena for persons to share their faith. Therefore the basic focus of Southern Baptist missions is the planting and nurturing of those churches.

"Church planting" is an interesting term. We usually talk of "building a church" or "organizing a church" or "constituting a church." "Planting" speaks of selecting acreage, tilling soil, sowing seeds, weeding around the young plants, protecting them from infestation, and harvesting fruit. It speaks of work and faith, of anticipation and potential, of positives and negatives. "Planting a *church*" speaks of God and people, similarities and varieties, individuals and groups.

In one sense all churches are alike. Christians from the United States traveling overseas are often amazed, as they visit churches, at the sense of rapport and fellowship they feel. In spite of some obvious differences they usually come away feeling a sense of kinship with those with whom they have worshipped. All churches exist under the Lordship of Christ and are brought into being by the power of God. They all take occasion to worship, study the Bible, proclaim the gospel and minister in the name of Christ. There is a great deal that is alike in church life everywhere.

In another sense each church is unique. Because Christ's saving work uniquely occurs in the life of each individual, the corporate life of groups of those individuals will not be exactly like any other group. Because churches seek to minister in their community, they build their programs according to the needs of their community. These programs will therefore differ from commu-

nity to community.

The way a church is started influences it for years, if not for all its life. Some churches are started by the vision of a mother church, some by a committed individual or family moving to a new community, some by church split and some in competition with a sister church.

The culture in which the church is planted both influences it and is influenced by it. Churches in an African culture differ from churches in a Japanese culture. Churches in Eastern Europe differ from churches in the United States. Churches in rural areas differ from church in urban areas.

The way it was started, the individuals who compose it, the culture in which it exists and the community to which it ministers all work to make each church unique.

God has used Baptists to plant these "alike but different" churches in many places and under many circumstances: in great cities such as Tokyo, Berlin, Lagos, Sao Paulo, Manila, Mexico City, Jerusalem and Nairobi; among nomadic tribal people in Africa and Asia; among remote villages in Guatemala, Thailand, Bangladesh, Tanzania and Indonesia; in responsive places such as Korea, the Philippines, Nigeria, and Brazil; in difficult and slow places like Jordan, Senegal and Malaysia.

Some of these churches study and worship in magnificent buildings, some in primitive huts, some under the spread of large trees and some in homes. At least one exists in a prison!

Church Planting

As we reflect on the churches we have looked at in this book,

Photograph on pages 78-79:

In Tamale, Ghana, the Baptist Training Centre prepares a steady stream of men and women to help start churches and become pastors and church leaders. Missionary Ralph Davis, principal, and Abdul Karimu, assistant principal, oversee leadership training.

what conclusions do we draw?

What does it mean to *plant* a church in another country?

Church planting is not a cultural process. The object of Southern Baptist missionaries in planting churches in another land is not to recreate a bit of American culture on "foreign soil." Just as Southern Baptist churches reflect the culture in which they exist, so churches in other lands reflect their culture. Worship styles and hymnody will reflect the styles of that culture. If the dominant musical pattern is drums, gongs, simple reeds or stringed instruments, music in the church will follow those patterns. Wor-

Missionary Wendell Smith, left, finds his home a convenient location for TEE (Theological Education by Extension) classes.

ship may be sedate, as in Switzerland, or casual and exuberant, as in Kenya.

There are, for example, no Southern Baptist churches in Brazil—only Brazilian Baptist churches, flourishing in their own culture.

Worship patterns vary according to culture. In Indonesia worshippers may sit on mats on the floor with men on one side of the room and women on the other. The worship leader may sit on the floor along with the worshippers. In Singapore the churches

Home Bible study as a step in church planting is effective in areas open to the gospel as well as in those where it is more difficult to establish churches. Mrs. Chang Young Shim visits with Mrs. Kim Young Mae at Mrs. Kim's home in Seoul, Korea, a country where church growth is dramatic.

Juan Pedro Maldonado (far right) starts at the beginning of the cycle of church planting as he witnesses in the municipal park in Elche, Spain.

may gather on a Thursday evening for prayer; in Korea all the churches gather each morning at 4:30 for prayer time.

If persons in other cultures are to be attracted to the churches planted in their land, those churches must not appear foreign to them. A wise Vietnamese Christian said many years ago that three things brand a religion as foreign to the Vietnamese culture: the architecture of its house of worship, its organizational structure, and its worship style and hymnody. The church should not seem foreign to any culture. Christ founded the church in a Mideast culture and fully intended that it should be planted in every culture with each giving unique expression to it.

Church planting is not an organizational transfer. Missionaries are not attempting to reproduce a Southern Baptist church organizational structure overseas. WMU, Brotherhood, Sunday School, Church Training, choir programs and other organizations have developed in Southern Baptist life to meet specific needs expressed by Southern Baptists and Southern Baptist churches. Organizational structures will emerge in churches overseas through that same dynamic. As needs are identified and as perceptive leaders shape structures to meet those needs, organizational patterns will emerge.

Every church will surely emphasize missions, training and Bible study; but the way they organize those efforts may be quite different from the way they are organized in the United States. In fact, the way they organize to meet those needs in Liberia will be quite different from the way they organize to meet them in Chile. We should not be surprised if we find no WMU or Brotherhood in churches overseas, though we would be chagrined if there were no plan of any kind to emphasize missions among the Christians in the churches.

Church planting is not a casual and careless avocation. Seeds carelessly sown at random seldom bear maximum fruit. Great care must be taken in the preparation of the soil, the sowing, the watering, the weeding and the harvest.

Since so much of church planting is culturally oriented it is best done by those persons who can minister effectively within that culture. Local Baptist leaders are trained and move easily and productively within their own cultural pattern. But missionaries also are able to minister effectively in cultures other than their own.

Missionary John David Hopper (center) maintains communication with Eastern European Baptists and is impressed with the spiritual vitality of Baptist churches he visits. Here he is at First Baptist Church, Bucharest, Romania, with Pavel Barbatei (left), general secretary of the Romanian Baptist Union, and Cornel Mara, president of the union and pastor of the church.

To plant churches, there must be not only the planting of the gospel seed but also the planting of lives. This is no casual process. The missionary calling is the unmistakable call of God; it includes commitment to language learning and to cultural assim-

ilation. This is no short process. For missionaries to be effective
in church planting, they must accept and be accepted by the
people. Most missionaries feel this process really begins to bear
fruit during their second term of service—somewhere after four
or five years of diligently working out their calling in that culture.

This planting of life within a culture is often called "incarnational missions." Missionaries in whose life Christ is incarnate
plant themselves in a culture to be the incarnational expression of
Christ within that culture.

After missionaries establish a strong base of identification with
the people in that culture and local leaders emerge, the scene is
then set for short-term volunteer ministries. These ministries
have proven to be most effective as they relate to these local Baptist leaders and missionaries who have laid foundations and
whose commitment is to "see it through."

Church planting is basically a transformational process.
Church planting happens as lives are changed by the power of the
gospel. Outlook is changed and un-Christian aspects of a culture
are dropped by those transformed by the gospel.

Because church planting is transforming, it is a spiritual process. Spiritual processes require spiritual resources. Although this
is not a book on prayer, no treatment of the patterns of church
planting is complete without an acknowledgment that this never
happens without prayer. One dimension of church planting that
is not optional is prayer. Unless there is prayer by the planter,
those who sent the planter out and those brothers and sisters with
whom the planter works, churches will not be planted no matter
how many other good things are done.

*Church planting also never happens without the movement
of the Holy Spirit in the lives of people—believers and non-
believers.* Church planting is a divine process using human instruments. Christ said, "I will build my church" (Matt. 16:18). Church
planting is a process in which Christ continues to be active in his

These new students being greeted at Baptist Bible School, Rungwe, Tanzania, will soon help to establish churches.

Henry Ong, pastor of New Life Baptist Church in Singapore, shares a deep concern for the salvation of his countrymen. Their outreach has resulted in the birth of many new Christians and churches.

world, building his church. The activities of the instruments (the planters) only bring results as they become means whereby the Christ of the church is active through them.

What kind of church does one wish to see come out of church planting efforts? Simply put, the desire is to see a mature church. It's not easy to describe a mature church, but this sentence does it well: "A mature church is one that exists for others and can take care of itself."

The mature church has become neither ingrown nor introverted. It is rightly concerned for its own needs—to "take care of itself"—but this concern is not all-consuming. The mature church has learned how to share its financial resources. Social concern is evident as love for one's neighbor is worked out in a tangible way. A mature church is successfully discipling the non-Christians in its own community and is involved in cross-cultural missions for planting churches in other cultures.

A mature church doesn't have an inferiority complex. It is neither a dependent child nor a rebellious adolescent—having left those stages of development behind. It has developed a feeling of belonging within the cultural ecology, even when still a very small minority. It doesn't feel it has to apologize to anyone for its existence.

A mature church should be able to take care of its own expenses. It can build and maintain its own building, provide leadership training and Biblical instruction for its members, develop ministries to the community, aggressively evangelize in its own community, and participate in spreading the gospel around the world.

So this church planting process goes on. Not cultural, organizational, casual or careless, but powered by the purpose and presence of God. The desired end is that what God has planted will grow, mature and become a reproductive part of his body!

Luke dramatically closes the Book of Acts by speaking of the "kingdom and teachings about Christ" moving on "unhinderedly." May this be evermore true in our day as the seed falls—everywhere.

Lewis I. Myers, Jr.

Lewis I. Myers, Jr. is director of Consultant Services at the Foreign Mission Board, Southern Baptist Convention. He has been at the board since 1977, when he resigned from missionary service to become associate director of the Overseas Division.

Appointed in 1960, Myers was a missionary to Vietnam, where he worked in evangelism and publications. On furlough when Vietnam fell in 1975, he was soon helping the Home Mission Board with their ministry to the Vietnamese.

Myers is a native Mississippian and a graduate of Mississippi College. He has a master of divinity degree from Southern Baptist Theological Seminary in Louisville, Kentucky. He and his wife, Toni, have four grown children.

Personal Learning Activities

1. Describe the "planting process" that resulted in Kathemboni Baptist Church. How is church planting a family affair in Kenya?

2. How does the name "Rural Life Center" capture the full dimension of this ministry? What does the acronym BOOST mean? Explain how church planting comes from this program.

3. What cultural barriers faced missionaries James and Beth Smith in Ashkelon? Explain how the Smith family planted a church in Ashkelon.

4. What method of church planting effective in Brazil is similar to the example in Israel? How did volunteers from the Untied States help with church planting in Brazil?

5. "Church planting is a divine process using human instruments." Elaborate on this quotation from the book.

Appropriate Responses
to a Study of Missions

My commitment: to the best of my ability and with God's help I will

( ) **Pray for missions and missionaries.**
For a prayer list and missions information refer to *The Commission, Open Windows, World Mission Journal, Probe, Royal Service, Contempo, Accent.*

( ) **Give to the annual Lottie Moon Christmas Offering for Foreign Missions, through my local church.**

( ) **Keep up with current foreign mission news.**
Subscribe to *The Commission* and magazines listed above.

( ) **Accept the call of God to become a missionary.**
For further information write to: Foreign Mission Board, Box 6767, Richmond, Virginia 23230.

( ) **Serve from two weeks to two years on a mission field as a volunteer.**
Write to the Foreign Mission Board, Box 6767, Richmond, Virginia 23230 for information about volunteer opportunities.

( ) **Encourage my church to increase our Cooperative Program giving.**

( ) **Include foreign missions in my will.**
For further information write to: Foreign Mission Board Treasurer, Box 6767, Richmond, Virginia 23230.

Signed _____ Date _____

(Keep this commitment record as a reminder.)

The Church Study Course

The Church Study Course is a Southern Baptist education system consisting of short courses for adults and youth combined with a credit and recognition system. Also available in the system are noncredit short courses (called foundational units) for children and preschoolers. The courses in the Church Study Course are for use in addition to the ongoing study and training curricula made available to churches by the denomination.

More than 500 courses are available in 23 subject areas. Courses are flexible enough to offer credit for either individual or group study. Credit is awarded for each course completed. These credits may be applied to one or more of the 100 plus diploma plans in the system. Diplomas are available for most leadership positions as well as general diplomas for all Christians. These diplomas are the certification that a person has completed from five to eight prescribed courses. Diploma requirements are given in the catalogs.

"Enrollment" in a diploma plan is made by completing Form 725 "Church Study Course Enrollment/Credit Request" and sending it to the Awards Office at the Sunday School Board. Course credit may also be requested on this form. A permanent record of courses and diplomas will be maintained by the Awards Office. Twice each year up-to-date reports called "transcripts" will be sent to churches to distribute to members participating in the Church Study Course. Each transcript will list courses and diplomas completed and will show progress toward diplomas currently being sought. The transcript will show which courses are needed to complete diploma requirements. A diploma will be issued automatically when the final requirement is met.

Complete details about the Church Study Course system, courses available, and diplomas offered may be found in a current copy of the *Church Study Course Catalog* and in the study course section of the *Church Materials Catalog*. Study course materials are available from Baptist Book Stores.

The Church Study Course system is simple enough to be administered by volunteer workers with limited time. The system is universal so that credit earned in one church is recognized in all other Southern Baptist churches. Approximately 600,000 awards are earned by adults and youth each year.

The Church Study Course is promoted by the Sunday School Board, 127 Ninth Avenue, North, Nashville, Tennessee 37234; by Woman's

Missionary Union, P.O. Box C-10, Birmingham, Alabama 35283-0010; by the Brotherhood Commission, 1548 Poplar Avenue, Memphis, Tennessee 38104; and by the respective departments of the state conventions affiliated with the Southern Baptist Convention.

How to Request Credit for this Course

This book is the text for course number 08098 in subject area: "Missions." This course is designed for 2½ hours of group study.

Credit for this course may be obtained in two ways:

1. Read the book and attend class sessions. (If you are absent from one or more sessions, complete the "Personal Learning Activities" for the material missed.)
2. Read the book and complete the "Personal Learning Activities." (Written work should be submitted to an appropriate church leader.)

A request for credit may be made on Form 725 "Church Study Course Enrollment/Credit Request" and sent to the Awards Office, Sunday School Board, 127 Ninth Avenue, North, Nashville, Tennessee 37234. The form on the following page may be used to request credit.

A record of your awards will be maintained by the Awards Office. Twice each year copies will be sent to churches for distribution to members.

Cut along dotted line

CHURCH STUDY COURSE
ENROLLMENT/CREDIT REQUEST (FORM-725)

INSTRUCTIONS:
1. Please PRINT or TYPE.
2. COURSE CREDIT REQUEST—Requirements must be met. Use exact title.
3. ENROLLMENT IN DIPLOMA PLANS—Enter selected diploma title to enroll.
4. For additional information see the Church Study Course Catalog.
5. Duplicate additional forms as needed. Free forms are available from the Awards Office and State Conventions.

TYPE OF REQUEST: (Check all that apply)

☐ Course Credit
☐ Enrollment in Diploma Plan

☐ Address Change
☐ Name Change
☐ Church Change

REQUEST FOR

☐ Mr. ☐ Miss
☐ Mrs.

DATE OF BIRTH ⬆

Month	Day	Year

Name (First, Mi, Last)

Street, Route, or P.O. Box

City, State, Zip Code

CHURCH

Church Name

Mailing Address

City, State, Zip Code

COURSE CREDIT REQUEST

Course No	Use exact title
08098	1. The Seed Is Sown
Course No	Use exact title
	2.
Course No	Use exact title
	3.
Course No	Use exact title
	4.
Course Nc	Use exact title
	5.

ENROLLMENT IN DIPLOMA PLANS

If you have not previously indicated a diploma(s) you wish to earn, or you are beginning work on a new one(s), select and enter the diploma title from the current Church Study Course Catalog. Select one that relates to your leadership responsibility or interest. When all requirements have been met, the diploma will be automatically mailed to your church. No charge will be made for enrollment or diplomas.

➡ Title of diploma | Age group or area
1.

➡ Title of diploma | Age group or area
2.

Signature of Pastor, Teacher, or Study Leader | Date

MAIL THIS REQUEST TO ⬆

CHURCH STUDY COURSE AWARDS OFFICE
RESEARCH SERVICES DEPARTMENT
127 NINTH AVENUE, NORTH
NASHVILLE, TENNESSEE 37234

FORM-725 (Rev 7-83)